Inside Special Operations™

CHEMICAL BIOLOGICAL INCIDENT RESPONSE FORCE

Janell Broyles

rosen publishing's
rosen
central

New York

Published in 2009 by The Rosen Publishing Group, Inc.
29 East 21st Street, New York, NY 10010
www.rosenpublishing.com

Library of Congress Cataloging-in-Publication Data

Broyles, Janell.
Chemical Biological Incident Response Force / Janell Broyles. — 1st ed.
    p.cm.—(Inside special operations)
Includes bibliographical references and index.
ISBN-13: 978-1-4042-1751-5 (lib. bdg.)
ISBN-13: 978-1-4358-5129-0 (pbk.)
6-pack ISBN-13: 978-1-4042-7860-8

1. United States. Marine Corps. Chemical Biological Incident Response Force—Juvenile literature. 2. Biological warfare—Juvenile literature. 3. Chemical warfare—Juvenile literature. 4. Emergency planning—United States—Juvenile literature. I. Title.
UG447.8.B77 2008
358'.344—dc22

                                                                    2007045127

Manufactured in Malaysia

On the cover: Hazardous materials experts case out the Hart Senate Office Building after an anthrax-laced letter was sent there in November 2001.

Contents

Local security forces in hazmat suits respond to the sarin attacks in Tokyo in 1995. Twelve people died in the attacks, which also caused severe disruptions in the Tokyo subway system while it was secured and decontaminated.

Introduction

In March 1995, the whole world watched in horror as Japanese civilians were killed and terrorized by an act of chemical warfare. Members of Aum Shinrikyo, a Japanese cult, released a deadly gas called sarin in the city of Tokyo. Targeting the Tokyo train system, five cult members carried packages of sarin into five different trains, punctured them to let the gas escape, and then got off at the next stop. Twelve victims died, and 5,500 other people were sickened or otherwise affected by the poisonous gas.

In the United States, a Marine Corps commandant, General Charles C. Krulak, went to his commander and asked what the Marine Corps' Pacific Command could do to assist the Japanese. The answer was brief and disappointing: "We've got nothing." Determined to do better than that, General Krulak established the Chemical Biological Incident Response Force, or CBIRF, the following July. By April 1996, the new force was operational.

According to author Chris Seiple, CBIRF's unique and fleet-footed organization, structure, and goals made it a "revolutionary organization." Created out of existing U.S. Marine forces and resources, CBIRF's responsibilities includes reconnaissance, detection, decontamination, medical, security, and service support for managing crisis situations at home and abroad. CBIRF's stated mission is to "forward-deploy and/or respond to a credible threat of a Chemical, Biological, Radiological, Nuclear, or High Yield explosive (CBRNE) incident in order to assist local, state, or federal agencies and Unified Combat Commanders in the conduct of consequence management operations." The official CBIRF Web site (http://cbirf.usmc.mil) goes on to say that its goals include "providing capabilities for agent detection and identification; casualty search, rescue, and personnel decontamination; and emergency medical care and stabilization of contaminated personnel."

General Charles C. Krulak

Born in 1942, Charles Chandler Krulak served as the 31st commandant of the Marine Corps from 1995 to 1999. His father served in World War II, Korea, and Vietnam. Krulak graduated from the U.S. Naval Academy in 1964 with a bachelor's degree, and he went on to get a master's degree in labor relations from George Washington University. Krulak held many commanding officer positions, including that of a platoon and two rifle companies in Vietnam; the Counterguerrilla Warfare School in Okinawa, Japan; and the 3rd Battalion, 3rd Marines.

Krulak was assigned duty as the deputy director of the White House Military Office in September 1987. While serving in this capacity, he was selected for promotion to brigadier general in November 1988. Krulak was advanced to major general on March 20, 1992, and promoted to lieutenant general on September 1, 1992. In March 1995, he was nominated to serve as the commandant of the Marine Corps and assumed duties as the 31st commandant on June 30, 1995. Following his retirement from the Marine Corps, Krulak became the chief administrative officer for MBNA America. During his long years of service, Krulak received many honors and decorations, including the Silver Star, the Bronze Star, and a Purple Heart.

A 1996 portrait of General Charles C. Krulak

A simpler description of CBIRF's mission is that it is a special marine unit of first responders. It is meant to be a well-trained, quick-moving group of soldiers, doctors, and scientists who can be mobilized to detect, prevent, or respond to terrorist threats or catastrophes that involve biological weapons, chemical weapons, or nuclear agents. Although responding to terrorist attacks and catastrophic accidents are two different missions, both scenarios require very similar skills. In addition, when some sort of event happens, like the anthrax attacks of 2001, it is not always clear right away whether it was an attack or an accident. CBIRF is authorized to respond to either one so that no time is lost in containing the danger and reducing the risks to civilians.

In our current chaotic, destabilized, and threatening global environment, organizations like CBIRF that have multiple roles are absolutely critical. In the following chapters, we will look at how the group is organized, how it operates, the men and women who make it up, and what its future may be.

1. Responding to Terror

Even before the 1995 Aum Shinrikyo attacks in Tokyo, Japan, chemical and biological warfare had been a grave concern for the United States and other nations. Technology and science are changing our world, in many ways for the better. However, this high-tech boom means that sharing information and creating more powerful weapons are also easier than they once were.

Biological and chemical warfare first became a widespread threat when modern techniques of weaponizing germs and chemicals began to be developed in the early twentieth century. The ability to manipulate viruses and bacteria in the laboratory meant more effective cures were found for common diseases. But it also meant that those germs could be made even more deadly. Likewise, great strides were made in the nineteenth and early twentieth centuries toward understanding how chemicals were constructed and how they could be put into new combinations. However, along with these discoveries came the power to create new and deadly poisons in great quantities that could be used as weapons of war.

From World War I to the Cold War

In World War I, mustard gas, or chloroethyl sulfide, was a common form of chemical weapon. It blistered the skin and burned the lungs of its victims. Other "weapon" gases included chlorine, hydrogen cyanide, and chloropicrin, all of which damaged skin, eyes, lungs, and other tissues, killing or crippling those who were exposed to them. Biological warfare was still relatively crude in World War I, mostly consisting of attempts to infect livestock that would be used by enemy forces with diseases like glanders and anthrax. After the war, the Geneva Protocol banned the use of chemical and biological weapons, and their use declined.

In World War II, however, all sides in the global conflict experimented with forms of biological weapons. Japan used them extensively, mostly during its attacks on China. Japanese troops attempted to spread plague, anthrax, cholera, and other diseases as a way of weakening Chinese resistance. Chemical and biological weapons proved to be of limited use, however. In conventional battle, both kinds of weapons are difficult to control; a shift in the wind can mean that your own

Like these British soldiers wounded by German gas attacks, many soldiers were blinded or otherwise injured by chemical weapons used during World War I.

troops are just as likely to be affected as enemy troops. Also, some agents linger in soil and water, making the land unsafe for the victors.

It was not until the Cold War that biological and chemical weapons again generated interest, especially for the two world superpowers, the United States and the Soviet Union. Weapons of terror, which could be used to cripple enemy civilians and infrastructure without risking the lives of one's own ground troops, gained new appeal. It was believed that if a full-scale war finally erupted between the United States and Soviet Union, nuclear war would be the inevitable result, and both sides would lose. But if a good enough bioweapon or chemical weapon could be found, the reasoning went, it could be used to less devastating effect.

More important, each side did not want to have fewer or less powerful weapons than the other, and thus appear vulnerable and inferior. So if one superpower began stock-piling chemical and biological weapons, the other side would have to follow suit. Both sides poured their resources into creating these weapons and creating defenses against them. Fortunately, neither side ever decided to use them.

The Rise of Terrorism

The Cold War finally ended in the early 1990s, with the fall of the Berlin Wall, the reunification of Germany, and the collapse of the Soviet Union. However, with these promising developments came new and equally grave threats. Small states and terrorist groups, many of them with grievances against the United States, western European nations, Israel, or Russia, began to use terrorist tactics against their enemies. Their weapons included explosives, guerrilla attacks, hostage-taking, and other forms

This undated photo shows a Hamas suicide bomber named Izzedine al-Masri posing with the Koran and an M-16 rifle. On August 9, 2001, al-Masri blew himself up in a Jerusalem pizzeria, killing fifteen people. Suicide bombing remains one of the bloodiest and most effective weapons of terrorist groups.

of disruption against those whom they saw as oppressors and occupiers.

These terrorist groups had no large armies, tanks, or planes, but they had ingenuity and determination. In fact, fighting terrorism is not about who has the most powerful weapons. Many weapons of terror are merely crude explosives. What makes them terrorizing is that they are used in crowds of civilians, deliberately set off to hurt the most vulnerable and innocent members of the civilian population.

This doesn't mean, however, that terrorist groups wouldn't use stronger weapons if they could obtain them. After the Cold War, many in the West became concerned that the states of the former Soviet Union, which were going through economic and political upheaval, were not guarding their nuclear, chemical, and biological weapons and material well enough. Western countries continue to worry about radical groups who might seek to buy or steal these materials for use in terrorist attacks.

As the fight against terrorism escalated, the appeal to terrorists of more devastating weapons that did more harm only increased. Terrorists who could make their own chemical or biological weapons, or obtain nuclear material, would be able to cause enormous amounts of fear and panic.

Terrorists hide in the civilian population, they don't wear uniforms, and they strike without warning. To fight an enemy such as that requires intelligence, advanced detection tools, quick response, and preparation for any kind of attack or catastrophic event.

Domestic Terrorism

Terrorists do not have to be "outsiders" or foreigners. While most Americans still think of the September 11, 2001, attacks by Al Qaeda against U.S. targets when they think of terrorism, there have been several instances of domestic, or "homegrown," terrorist acts. These include the Oklahoma City bombing in 1995, the Atlanta Olympics bombing in 1996, and the anthrax attacks of 2001 to 2002.

This photo taken on the day of the bombing shows the north side of the devastated Alfred P. Murrah Federal Building in Oklahoma City. The attack, carried out by Timothy McVeigh, was the worst terrorist attack on U.S. soil prior to the attacks of September 11, 2001.

In every war, soldiers and civilians alike have been among the casualties. But in the age of terrorism, civilians are not secondary targets or accidental casualties—they are the principal targets. The murder of innocent citizens is the primary goal of most terrorist acts. To fight terrorism, the modern military has to be able to respond anywhere that civilians live and to coordinate with local responders like the police, the fire department, the Coast Guard, and others to contain and minimize the effect of an attack. That is where the Chemical Biological Incident Response Force (CBIRF) has focused its efforts.

2. Detection, Protection, Response

Since April 1996, the Chemical Biological Incident Response Force's original role has expanded. According to the SpecialOperations.com Web site, it currently consists of approximately 350 to 375 marines and sailors from a variety of military occupational specialties. This site goes on to note that "CBIRF is most effective when forward-deployed in response to a credible threat or to protect events of national significance." Some of CBIRF's capabilities now include chemical and biological agent detection and identification, hazard prediction, advanced life saving and triage, evacuation of victims from contaminated areas, decontamination, incident site management, and security.

CBIRF's Mission and Chain of Command

The direction of CBIRF ultimately rests with the Department of Defense (DOD). The DOD is the federal department charged with coordinating and supervising all agencies and functions of the government relating directly to national security and the military. Housed at the Pentagon in Arlington, Virginia, the DOD oversees the U.S. Army, Navy, Air Force, and Marine Corps, as well as noncombat agencies such as the National Security Agency and the Defense Intelligence Agency.

Officially, CBIRF is part of the II Marine Expeditionary Force (IIMEF), which consists of ground, air, and logistics forces that can sustain themselves in combat without assistance for up to sixty days. The II Marine Expeditionary Force is commanded by a lieutenant general, who serves under the commander of the U.S. Marine Corps Forces Command, which provides marine fighting formations and units to the European Command, Central Command, and Southern Command.

In the aftermath of the September 11, 2001, terrorist attacks on the United States, CBIRF's mission became incorporated into

This aerial photo of the Pentagon was taken in September 2003. The Pentagon is the highest-capacity office building in the world. It houses approximately 23,000 military and civilian employees and about 3,000 non-defense support personnel.

the 4th MEB, along with the Marine Security Force Battalion, the Marine Security Guard Battalion, and a new antiterrorism battalion. An MEB, or Marine Expeditionary Brigade, is the lead echelon of an expeditionary force, usually put together for a specific task. The 4th MEB was created to respond to crises worldwide within seventy-two hours. Training in the 4th MEB focuses on urban-warfare skills, marksmanship, and the ability to deal with nuclear, biological, and chemical threats.

Since the 2001 terrorist attacks and the resulting U.S. and allied war on Afghanistan and Iraq, such units have become more common. The military skills and services that CBIRF offers are even more important in a climate where the enemy may be using unconventional as well as conventional weapons. In fact, according to an article in *National Defense Magazine,* CBIRF forces are in high demand and have a difficult time keeping up with the military's deployment needs.

CBIRF members work in about forty different specialties. Additionally, it has its own science and technology shop, and an "interagency liaison cell"—troops who are kept in close communication with domestic agencies during emergencies and special events. CBIRF also includes two board-certified emergency-room physicians who will venture into any contaminated areas. Ninety CBIRF members are commissioned to serve on one-hour notice. An additional two hundred are on four-hour notice, as a reserve backup force.

In general, while CBIRF is a part of the military, it often takes orders from local or federal civilian authorities, whose perspective on events is often the most accurate and effective. According to CBIRF colonel T. X. Hammes, quoted in *National Defense Magazine*, "We are a consequence management organization. We only show up when we are invited, not on our own." Writing in the Marine Corps magazine *Leatherneck*, Margaret Bone described CBIRF this way: "It's new, it's unique to the Armed Services, and right now, it's the only quick reaction force in the world equipped to help in the aftermath of a chemical, biological, or radiological [nuclear] attack."

Organizations That Partner with CBIRF

FEMA (Federal Emergency Management Agency)

Mission: To coordinate the response to a disaster that has occurred in the United States and that overwhelms the resources of local and state authorities.

U.S. National Guard

Mission: To be mobilized at any time by presidential order to supplement regular armed forces and upon declaration of a state of emergency by the governor of the state or territory in which they serve.

Army Technical Escort Unit (TEU)

Mission: To help in the removal, storage, and destruction of non-stockpile chemical weapons, to clean up military sites, and to detect weapons of mass destruction.

FBI (Federal Bureau of Investigation)

Mission: To protect and defend the United States against terrorist and foreign intelligence threats, to uphold and enforce the criminal laws of the United States, and to provide leadership and criminal justice services to federal, state, municipal, and international agencies and partners.

CIA (Central Intelligence Agency)

Mission: To collect information that reveals the plans, intentions, and capabilities of adversaries of the United States, producing timely analysis to the president and other decision makers, and to conduct covert action at the direction of the president to preempt threats or achieve U.S. policy objectives.

Bone goes on to note that "CBIRF is not a counterterrorist group, and it's not direct-action oriented, though there is a security element of more than 120 Marines, with the capability to increase that strength as needed." According to an article posted on www.espionageinfo.com, a force protection element commander for CBIRF says, "Our mission is to respond, to come in and save lives. We bring the full package: self-contained, expeditionary, and task-organized."

CBIRF's Commanding Officers

CBIRF is an expertly skilled and lightning-fast reaction force. Its leaders, therefore, must be highly intelligent, courageous, motivational, detail oriented, and steady under intense pressure. The following profiles provide good insight into just how much

Evacuees from the October 2006 fires in California wait in line for FEMA assistance. FEMA is a partner with CBIRF, and its mission includes aiding those rendered homeless or injured by a terrorist attack as well as by a natural disaster.

goes into creating a CBIRF commander and exactly what it takes to be a leader of such an elite force.

Lieutenant Colonel Michael P. Rohlfs Jr.

Lieutenant Colonel Rohlfs currently serves as the commanding officer of CBIRF. He was commissioned in 1991 through the Naval Reserve Officer Training Course. Rohlfs was later sent on several deployments, including to Iraq. Rohlf's decorations include the Defense Meritorious Service Medal, Navy and Marine Corps Commendation Medal with two gold stars, and the Joint Achievement Medal.

Major Robert F. Piper III

Major Robert F. Piper III serves as the executive officer of CBIRF. His first tour as a regular officer for CBIRF was as the ground supply officer for the Marine Wing Support Group, during which he made two deployments in support of Operation Iraqi Freedom during the Second Gulf War in 2003 and 2004. His awards include the Navy Marine Corps Commendation Medal, the Naval Achievement Medal, the Combat Action Ribbon, and the Outstanding Volunteer Service Medal.

First Sergeant William R. Frye

First Sergeant William R. Frye serves as the battalion sergeant major of CBIRF. He joined CBIRF as the React Company first sergeant in January 2006. His awards include the Bronze Star Medal, Navy/Marine Commendation Medal with combat distinguishing device, Navy/Marine Corps Achievement Medal 5 Award, Outstanding Volunteer Medal, Combat Action Ribbon 3RD Award, and the Marine Corps Drill Instructor Ribbon.

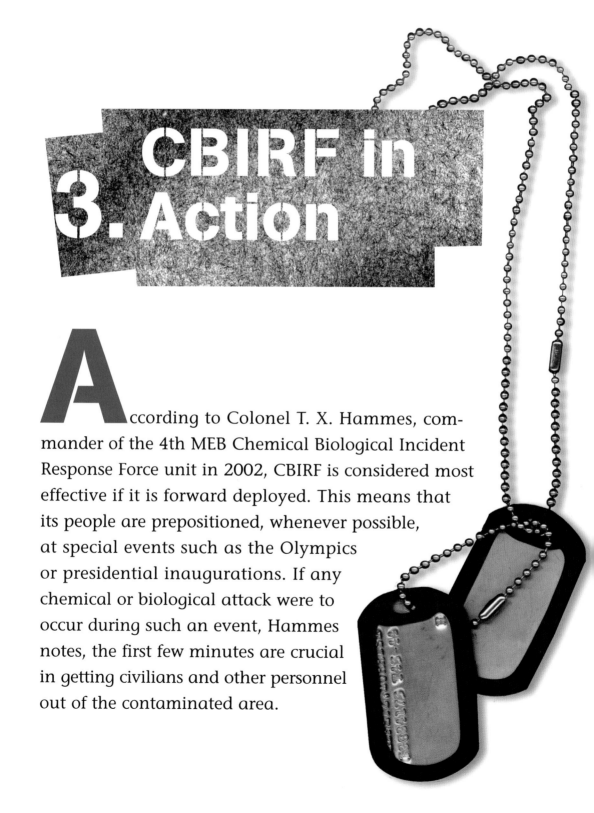

3. CBIRF in Action

According to Colonel T. X. Hammes, commander of the 4th MEB Chemical Biological Incident Response Force unit in 2002, CBIRF is considered most effective if it is forward deployed. This means that its people are prepositioned, whenever possible, at special events such as the Olympics or presidential inaugurations. If any chemical or biological attack were to occur during such an event, Hammes notes, the first few minutes are crucial in getting civilians and other personnel out of the contaminated area.

CBIRF members do not wear uniforms. According to Hammes, "We look like street vendors in civilian clothes." Once an incident happens, "We are ready in seven minutes to begin decontamination." Hammes also notes in his interview with *National Defense Magazine* that CBIRF nearly tripled its decontamination capabilities, from a rate of treating sixty-five casualties per hour to two hundred per hour, during 2002.

Hammes believes that one advantage that CBIRF has over most local first-responder agencies is that it trains more often. New York City, for instance, has the best emergency-response forces in the United States, he explains, but they train only once every six to twelve months because they cannot afford to be away from their home station.

As in all military operations, CBIRF's effectiveness is sometimes hampered by its access to adequate funding. In his interview with *National Defense Magazine*, Hammes notes that his unit was seeking new equipment like filters, cooling equipment, devices to transport casualties, and decontamination devices. "Currently, we are using Wal-Mart garden equipment," says Hammes.

Despite these obstacles, however, CBIRF proved itself both effective and critical to the defense of average Americans on two occasions—the 1996 Atlanta Olympics bombing and the 2001 anthrax attacks.

The 1996 Olympics Bombing

On July 27, 1996, after the sports events had ended for the day, fans attending the Summer Olympic Games in Atlanta, Georgia, continued to celebrate by listening to bands, dancing, and strolling around the city's picturesque Centennial Olympic Park.

Sometime after midnight, Eric Robert Rudolph set down a green military knapsack under a park bench and walked away. Inside were three pipe bombs surrounded by nails. Shortly thereafter, security guard Richard Jewell discovered the bag and alerted Georgia Bureau of Investigation officers. Nine minutes later, Rudolph called 911 to deliver a warning. Jewell and other security guards began clearing the immediate area so that a bomb squad could investigate the knapsack, but at 1:21 AM, the bomb exploded. One woman was killed by a nail, and a man died of a heart attack while running away. One hundred and eleven other people were injured in the explosion and its aftermath.

But it could have been much worse. Unknown to Rudolph and to most of those attending the Olympics, CBIRF, along with a host of other response teams and federal agents, had been training for terrorist activity at the games. CBIRF had correctly assumed that such an event would be a magnet for people like Rudolph or even foreign terrorist groups. Although

Bomb squad members check a suspicious package on an Atlanta street in August 1996. Because the attack at Olympic Centennial Park had taken place a few weeks prior, local authorities were still on high alert. The bomber, Eric Robert Rudolph, was not captured until May 2003.

it was later determined that Rudolph's attack used a very simple explosive without any traces of chemical, biological, or nuclear agents, first responders reacted the way they had been trained to by CBIRF: with the assumption that there might be a biological, chemical, or nuclear hazard.

Months before the Olympic Games, the Georgia Department of Natural Resources had brought CBIRF in to help train local first responders in meeting the challenges posed by a chemical or biological terrorist event. These local first responders, including the Atlanta Fire Department, performed drills with the Marine Corps' CBIRF before and during the Olympic events. Earlier

Atlanta firefighters train in first-response techniques in the months before the Atlanta Olympics. Here, an injured "passenger" is carried off a train on a stretcher after a staged attack. CBIRF was instrumental in preparing Atlanta's local responders.

that year, Donald Hiett Jr., assistant fire chief of the Atlanta Fire Department, put together an FBI-sponsored symposium on disaster medicine for chemical and biological terrorist incidents.

Hiett's department and other local first responders also joined federal and state agencies in a drill in Atlanta's subway system. Called "Olympic Charlie," the drill used surrogate (substitute and harmless) chemical agents to train participants how to respond to a terrorist attack in a crowded, enclosed space. Before these preparations, Atlanta firefighters had been trained to respond only to hazardous materials incidents, like chemical spills, but not terrorist incidents.

As it turned out, Atlanta firefighters were the first on the scene after the Rudolph bombing. But before Hiett arrived at the site, he called in CBIRF. Both groups arrived at the site

CBIRF-Monitored Events

Part of CBIRF's mission is to be ready to respond to threats during events of "national importance," also known as national special security events, or NSSEs. These have included:

- Olympic events
- Presidential State of the Union addresses and addresses to Joint Sessions of Congress
- Papal visits
- NATO 50th Anniversary Summit in April 1999
- Y2K New Year's celebration in January 2000
- Summit of Eight (G-8) Conference

For national security reasons, not all of CBIRF's missions are publicized. Having their headquarters in Indian Head, Maryland, close to Washington, D.C., allows them to respond quickly to threats against members of the government.

simultaneously. Once laboratory testing of the bomb site confirmed that there were no biological, chemical, or nuclear agents, however, the investigation was turned over to the FBI and local authorities. "Knowing we had CBIRF, we felt we were prepared" for a chemical or biological incident at the Olympics, says Hiett.

The 2001 Anthrax Attacks

One of the most terrifying—and still unsolved—cases of terrorist attacks ever to occur in the United States was the anthrax contaminations of 2001. Beginning on September 18, just one week after the infamous Al Qaeda attacks on the World Trade Center, the Pentagon, and Flight 93, letters containing deadly anthrax spores were mailed to several news media offices and two Democratic U.S. senators, killing five people and infecting and sickening seventeen others.

CBIRF swung into action, sending teams of incident response marines to the various offices, homes, and postal stations affected by the toxic mailings. While every member of the CBIRF teams knew exactly what to do and how to respond, for many if not most of them, this was their first real experience with potentially deadly carcinogenic weapons. They had drilled and trained and practiced, but now they were actually confronting a very real, very dangerous biological attack.

MedillNewsDC.com reported one CBIRF medical corps member who rushed to the congressional office buildings as saying, "We actually got called; we actually got to do something. I don't want to say we actually got to prove ourselves, but after going up to Capitol Hill, more people got to learn about us."

Workers pause before entering the Hart Senate Office Building in November 2001. CBIRF partnered with the Coast Guard and other agencies to clean up after the anthrax attacks of 2001.

Unlike most attack scenes that members of the armed forces face, this one was eerily still and quiet, the very opposite of the usual sensory overload of battle. Congressional offices had been evacuated in a hurry and stood deserted, even as office machines continued to glow and blink, paperwork rustled, and coffee and tea grew cold in abandoned mugs. Through this bizarre freeze frame wandered CBIRF team members, wearing hazmat (hazardous materials) suits and gas masks, and collecting air and particle samples, which would later be sent to the Environmental Protection Agency (EPA) for analysis. "It just looked like people up and left—just left everything as is . . . and it had an eerie feeling to it," the CBIRF medic said.

Besides collecting samples, the marines were also charged with decontaminating their own team and other workers on Capitol Hill. If a person entered a congressional office building, he or she had to be thoroughly washed upon leaving. A decontamination squad of fifteen marines wearing airproof suits sprayed diluted bleach or water on people who were exiting. The unit also removed contaminated mail from the P Street Postal Facility in Washington, another unusual task for the CBIRF marines.

It is this flexibility and skill in a range of emergency tasks that make CBIRF such a valuable crisis response tool. As Colonel Hammes put it in the MedillNewsDC.com article, "Give us a mission and we'll figure out how to do it." And they'll do it quickly. CBIRF units can be fully deployed within sixty minutes of an alarm call going out and can have a decontamination unit set up and running only eight minutes after arriving at an attack or accident scene. Hammes believes that it is the CBIRF's flexibility, large numbers, reconnaissance capabilities, and medical staff that set it apart from other biological and chemical agent response teams.

4. Becoming a Part of CBIRF

If your ultimate goal is to join CBIRF, you first have to join the U.S. Marine Corps or the U.S. Navy. While CBIRF is under marine command, you may enter the Incident Response Force via service in the navy. Not all careers available for members of the armed forces are available for marines. Marines do not offer medical careers or careers for chaplains; these are given over to the navy. If you want to specialize in either of those areas as well as serve in the CBIRF, you will need to become a sailor in the navy.

A group of U.S. Marine recruits wait to begin training exercises at Parris Island, South Carolina. These recruits are training with pugil sticks, which simulate the use of a rifle as a club in close-quarter fighting. Marines are some of the most highly trained members of the U.S. military.

Becoming a Marine

According to the Princeton Review's Web site, those who join the marines have to choose between two career paths: that of an enlisted marine or that of a commissioned officer. Enlistees make up the majority of the active-duty force (and also of CBIRF). Being one of the Marine Corps' eighteen thousand officers requires a higher level of education, training, and commitment, but it offers greater responsibility and increased career opportunities in return.

Becoming an enlisted marine requires you to graduate from high school, earn a passing score on the Armed Services Vocational Aptitude Battery (ASVAB), and make it through thirteen weeks of basic training (officers must pass this as well). Basic training (also known as boot camp) takes place on either Parris Island, South Carolina (for people living east of the Mississippi River), or in San Diego, California (for people living west of the Mississippi). The course is emotionally and physically demanding, but there are many potential rewards. One of them is that enlistees receive education benefits—including the option to participate in the GI Bill, which can pay more than $35,000 for college—which they can use to attend college during or following their service.

Becoming an officer can be achieved via several different routes, but every candidate must earn a four-year college degree and attend some version of Officer Candidate School (OCS). OCS is about twelve weeks long and is essentially a test of your ability to lead, learn, and last. Following OCS and commissioning, you become a marine second lieutenant and attend the Basic School (TBS) for six months where you learn the essential skills of a marine officer. Those who want to become officers can also attend the U.S. Naval Academy. College students can apply for commissions by participating in the Naval Reserve Officers Training Corps (NROTC) at their college.

College students can also become involved in the Platoon Leaders Course (PLC), which provides them with some college tuition assistance, while college graduates can pursue commissions by applying to OCS after earning their bachelor's degree. High school students can enlist after their graduation. They can also enter the Delayed Entry Program (DEP) while still in high school and pick their date of departure for boot camp and choose their military occupational specialty (MOS).

While women are not eligible to participate in combat positions (in infantry, artillery, or armor crews), all other roles are open to them in the marines, including most positions in CBIRF. Female officers attend OCS and TBS courses and go through boot camp, receiving the same training that every male enlistee receives.

The Marine Corps prides itself on being self-sufficient, training its own engineers, computer programmers, lawyers, meteorologists, military police officers, news reporters, and accountants. The acquisition of technical skills in the Marine Corps, from Web design to aircraft maintenance, gives its members valuable experience for use both inside and outside the military. The Marine Corps gives its recruits ample opportunities for hands-on work, as well as enormous responsibility. Much is offered to them in terms of training, skills, and expertise, and much is expected in return.

The Marine Corps has a tight-knit mindset, seeing itself as a small, elite group within the military. The range of initial time commitment for a new recruit is four to six years, with the ability to stay on and serve for shorter periods of time afterward. NROTC graduates who received scholarships typically owe five years of service to the navy, as do U.S. Naval Academy graduates.

Women are becoming increasingly valued as members of the armed services.

There is a complex rank system for enlisted marines and commissioned officers. Marine officers tend to move up according to the following schedule: from second lieutenant to first lieutenant after two years, captain after four years, major after ten years, lieutenant colonel after sixteen years, colonel after twenty-two years, and the general officer ranks at some point thereafter. Enlisted marines begin as privates, privates first class, and lance corporals, before advancing to corporals, sergeants, staff sergeants, gunnery sergeants, first sergeants (or master sergeants), and sergeants major (or master gunnery sergeants). Advancement depends upon your abilities, time served in your rank, time spent in the service, the needs of the Corps, and your military occupational specialty. Generally speaking, rising through the ranks in the Marine Corps takes longer than it does in the army, since fewer spots become available in the former over the same period of time.

The pay is standard among the military branches, and each promotion brings a pay raise. In addition, marines are provided medical benefits, housing allowances, and other benefits that increase the value of the service. Many benefits and allowances increase with rank, so, for example, a major receives more money for housing than a first lieutenant does.

Joining the Navy

As with the Marine Corps, there are two career paths in the navy: as an officer and as an enlisted sailor. Officers require more training and a college degree, but they earn a higher salary. On the other hand, the CBIRF is made up mostly of enlisted marines and sailors, so you may actually find it easier to join CBIRF if you aren't an officer.

If you do decide to pursue an officer's patch, you will need to attend either a naval academy, which has extremely rigorous entrance requirements, or a college with an NROTC program.

Whichever program you choose, you will receive financial assistance for your education, receive military training during college, and graduate as an ensign, owing from five to nine years of service to the navy.

The requirements for enlisting in the navy are a high school diploma or equivalent and passing grades on exams that ensure that you're mentally, physically, and morally capable of enduring the rigors of military service. As with all the military branches, one of these tests is the Armed Services Vocational Aptitude Battery (ASVAB). Navy boot camp takes place at the Great Lakes Naval Training Center near Chicago, Illinois, and lasts for eight weeks. Your beginning enlisted rank is an E-1, or seaman recruit, with the chance to climb a rank every couple of years.

Along with your training and room and board while on active naval duty, you'll receive thirty days of vacation each year. You and your family will get free medical care and discounted insurance, as well as other benefits. One benefit is provided by the Montgomery G.I. Bill, which requires that you pay $100 a month for the first twelve months of enlistment, but it then gives you $23,400 toward a degree program when your active duty is finished. All enlistees who earn a college degree are eligible to apply to Officer Candidate School, complete the thirteen-week program, and become officers.

CBIRF Equipment

When CBIRF initially formed, it had a small budget and was often forced to make do with "off-the-shelf" equipment adapted from existing supplies and often featuring duct tape or other improvised modifications. According to the Web site Globalsecurity.org, this early equipment included mission oriented protective posture (MOPP) suits and M40 gas masks. Since then, CBIRF has acquired more sophisticated equipment, such as:

- XM-93 Fox: a nuclear, biological, and chemical (NBC) reconnaissance vehicle capable of detecting both vapor and liquid contamination
- Chemical agent monitors (CAMs)
- M256 detection kits for detecting vapor agents
- M8 and M9 paper for detecting liquid agents
- M21 remote sensing chemical agent automatic alarm (RSCAAL) for long-range chemical detection
- M258 decontamination kits

CBIRF is also a testing group for chemical- and biological-related equipment, techniques, procedures, and doctrine in the Marine Corps. It used to train military personnel worldwide in how to deal with chemical and biological threats, including nerve agents, like sarin gas; blister agents, like mustard gas; and biological threats, like anthrax and typhoid. CBIRF's equipment is capable of detecting, classifying, and identifying all known chemical and biological agents. If a unit is unable to identify an agent with its equipment, members are able to collect samples for later study.

Being the first personnel to enter an affected area, each CBIRF member may carry as much as 70 pounds (31.8 kilograms) of gear while wearing full protective garments and gas masks. To build their stamina, CBIRF units practice performing daily tasks in full MOPP gear. The unit carries M870 shotguns, M16-A2 service rifles, M-203 40 mm grenade launchers, M-249 squad automatic weapons, and M-204G medium machine guns. If necessary, they can shoulder weapons such as the 81 mm mortar and shoulder-launched, multipurpose assault weapon (SMAW), known as the "bunker buster."

CBIRF medical personnel use a variety of medical equipment. They also have two 997 high-mobility, multipurpose wheeled vehicles with advanced life support equipment. CBIRF also uses five-ton trucks, logistic vehicle systems (LVSs), and high-mobility, multipurpose wheeled vehicles (Humvees). These vehicles' inventory includes reverse osmosis water purification units (ROWPUs) and a variety of generators and forklifts, all of which allow them to operate for up to two weeks in foreign terrain.

Joining CBIRF

Whichever path you choose to becoming a marine or a navy sailor, you will need to develop the right specialized skills during your military training to be considered for CBIRF. Most of CBIRF's personnel are infantry "grunts," or all-around servicepeople with the usual basic and general skills. However, team members also usually come to master at least one of forty-three different career specialties, including weather, counterintelligence, explosive ordnance disposal, and public affairs. This array of expertise and experience makes CBIRF one of the most diverse and skilled military units in all of the armed forces.

You will most likely receive on-the-job training, based on the exam scores you receive in your chosen specialty. If you already know which area of expertise you wish to pursue, it might be a good idea to talk to marine recruiters, research colleges with NROTC programs, or do your own research online or at the library so that you have a clear idea of the academic requirements and other challenges ahead.

Regardless of their chosen career specialties, all marines and sailors who join the CBIRF go through the two-week CBIRF basic-training course. The course includes training in operating in confined spaces, search techniques, and the wearing of personal protective equipment. Completion of this crash course is followed by about a year of on-the-job training that

CBIRF members, along with local police, fire departments, and USMC personnel, complete a training exercise at Washington College in Chestertown, Maryland.

culminates in a week of additional intensive instruction with live chemical and biological agents.

CBIRF members learn to work with many other organizations and specialists, including U.S. Coast Guard personnel, police officers, and firefighters. The CBIRF training facility is even named after Deputy Chief Raymond Downey, the former commander of the New York City Fire Department's Special Operations Command. Deputy Chief Downey, a former marine, was helping CBIRF put together its rescue training program before he was killed during rescue operations at the World Trade Center on 9/11.

According to U.S. Northern Command News, former CBIRF commander Colonel Michael Campbell says it's a matter of "not if, but when" the CBIRF team will be needed next. To be better prepared for that day, one-third of CBIRF's marines are qualified as emergency medical technicians.

CBIRF's marines and sailors are divided among three companies: two initial response force companies, a headquarters, and a service company. At any given time, one IRF company, plus a supporting "slice" from the headquarters company, is on a short recall status; everyone else is on a longer recall status. That means personnel are limited as to how far they may travel from the CBIRF installation in Indian Head, Maryland. CBIRF's close proximity (about twenty-six miles [forty-two kilometers]) to the District of Columbia is important for responding to any attacks against the capitol.

CBIRF will always carry out its missions in support of a lead agency, Campbell says. And, unlike many other soldiers who witness and necessarily participate in extremely violent and deadly missions, CBIRF personnel are directly involved in the saving of lives and the prevention of illness, death, and destruction. "We'll never be in charge. That's a hard thing for marines. I tell these grunts who just came from the school of infantry, 'Just park your rifle. And oh, by the way, you'll never be in charge. You're not going to kill anybody. Heck, you're not going to hurt anybody. Your job is to save a life.'"

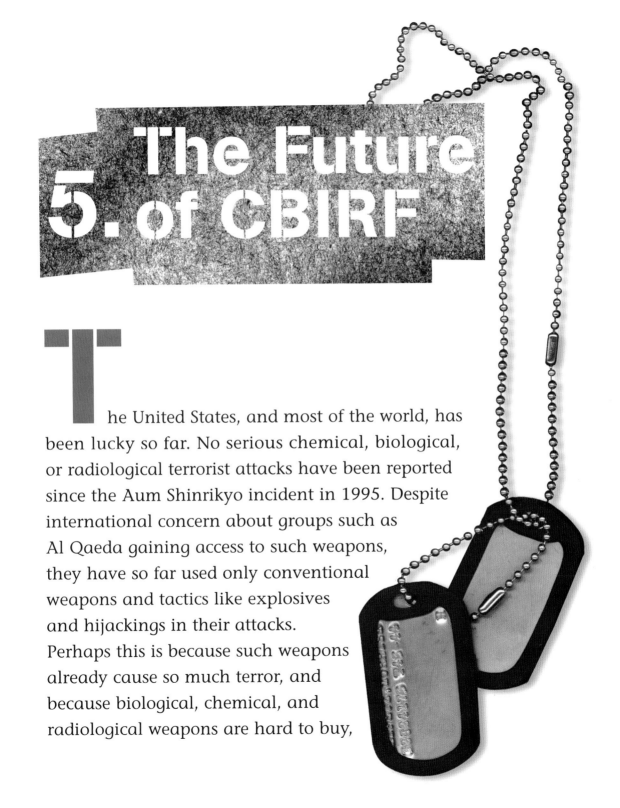

The Future 5. of CBIRF

The United States, and most of the world, has been lucky so far. No serious chemical, biological, or radiological terrorist attacks have been reported since the Aum Shinrikyo incident in 1995. Despite international concern about groups such as Al Qaeda gaining access to such weapons, they have so far used only conventional weapons and tactics like explosives and hijackings in their attacks. Perhaps this is because such weapons already cause so much terror, and because biological, chemical, and radiological weapons are hard to buy,

In a video released by Osama bin Laden, members of Al Qaeda brandish weapons. Bin Laden and supporters often release similar tapes as a way of taunting enemies and squashing rumors that bin Laden has died or been captured.

make, or transport, and pose a danger to anyone who handles them.

Identifying Possible Threats

Those who carry out terrorist acts often do not care about logic or about losing their own lives. The danger these kinds of fanatical terrorists pose cannot be ignored, especially since hazardous materials are getting easier to come by.

In October 2007, the Associated Press reported that the Defense Science Board, a panel of retired military and CIA officials and defense industry experts, was concerned that old hospital irradiation machines could be used to create radioactive "dirty" bombs. The panel urged the U.S. government to replace more than one thousand irradiation machines used in hospitals and research facilities. Such machines are relatively unguarded and contain cesium-137, one of the most dangerous and long-lasting radioactive materials. They are used for

Los Angeles police officers take part in a simulated dirty bomb attack in 2004 at the Port of Los Angeles. Because it is impossible to thoroughly inspect all containers coming ashore, port security is one of the biggest concerns in a terrorist attack.

radiation therapy and to sterilize blood and food. According to the board's members, "Any one of these 1,000-plus sources could shut down twenty-five square kilometers [9.7 square miles], anywhere in the United States, for forty-plus years [until decontamination is complete]."

Since 9/11, members of Congress and many citizen and military groups have also agitated for better protection for ports, chemical factories, nuclear facilities, food-processing operations, and oil refineries, all of which could be tempting targets for an enemy who wishes to cause widespread destruction. There have even been calls to build walls across the entire U.S.–Mexico border, which stretches for hundreds of miles, out of concern

Buggy Chemical Detectors

CBIRF has some of the most sophisticated mechanical equipment ever invented to sniff out chemicals in the air, soil, or water. But even the best human-made equipment is crude compared to living things that have evolved sensitive sensory receptors over many millennia. This is why so many safety patrols use drug- or bomb-sniffing dogs. And this is why some of the most sophisticated chemical-detection tools we have may be plants and bugs.

According to a 2003 *WIRED* article, Penn State scientists are developing "sentinel plants" that are genetically engineered to detect biological agents. The scientists believe that plants develop such good detection and chemical response protections because they are rooted in their environment and cannot escape from any dangerous situations that may arise. Many of these responses can be observed, such as changes in color, shape, or growth rate. By using technology to manipulate the plants' DNA, scientists hope to grow a plant that will respond in a visible way to chemical or biological agents. For example, the plants could turn brown, or even a fluorescent color, when they detect an agent in the soil, air, or water through their leaves or roots.

Other techniques involve using bees or other insects that have been trained to respond to certain scents. Investigators put a sample of material to be tested into a container with an insect that will fly or react in a certain way if it's a scent it has been trained to respond to. According to a 2006 *ScienceDaily* article, if rewarded with sugary water, wasps can be trained in just a few minutes to follow specific smells. The sensors in their antennae can detect chemicals in the air in tiny concentrations, much smaller than any human-made equipment can manage. And although dogs are also great scent detectors, insects have them beat in other ways. According to the scientist interviewed in the article, "The advantages of a wasp over a dog is you can produce them by the thousands. They are real inexpensive, and you can train them in a matter of minutes."

that terrorists could sneak into the United States at any of its weak, poorly guarded points.

It is hard to know how likely it is that the government will be able to take such drastic steps, however. Every one of these protective measures is very expensive and may require manpower and resources that even the United States doesn't possess. It is impossible to adequately protect every possible terrorist target without shutting down industry or severely curtailing the freedoms of the American people. Instead, the Department of Homeland Security and other agencies will likely continue to invest in training personnel such as those in CBIRF to respond to any possible emergency or attack.

Readiness to Respond

During times of war and upheaval, the risk of terrorism rises. Strong-arm dictators and fanatical rebels who seek more power, religious extremism that causes unrest and oppression, and an increase in poverty and violence caused by war all feed into the creation of terrorist groups. Poverty, anger, frustration, despair, and political oppression are all excellent seeds of terrorism, and the world has no shortage of displaced people, social outcasts, and political victims who are vulnerable to the false promise of justice offered by the gun and the bomb.

Terrorism did not end after 9/11 and the subsequent anthrax attacks. Although the United States has so far been spared another attack, bombings in Spain, England, and Pakistan, as well as violence in Myanmar (Burma) and Darfur highlight the fact that very real terrorist dangers exist worldwide. And, of course, the United States is currently embroiled in a war with Iraq that involves a great deal of enemy terrorist tactics. Whatever the outcome of these conflicts, it is clear that being able to respond quickly to any use of chemical, biological, or radiological weapons is critical.

CBIRF is really only one small part of that effort, an effort that includes many other military units—the Department of Homeland Security, CIA, FBI, NSA (National Security Agency), and the Coast Guard, among others. And one of CBIRF's strengths is that it doesn't see itself as a sole responder but as part of a team that includes all of these elements, as well as civilians. After all, it was just an ordinary civilian security guard named Richard Jewell who noticed the suspicious backpack at the Atlanta Olympics and set in motion the lifesaving chain of response-and-rescue events. It was an Atlanta assistant fire chief who coordinated his city's training with CBIRF and who made sure they would be there to respond when an emergency happened.

Emergency rescuers at work after the train bombings in Madrid, Spain, in 2004. The total number of victims was 191, coming from seventeen different countries.

And, according to its former commander, CBIRF itself is composed mostly of "regular grunts" who aren't looking for glory but for a chance to make a difference. No matter what challenges terrorism or accidental disaster will pose for the United States in the future, it's the work of fast-acting, trained, and dedicated responders that will make all the difference in terms of lives saved and catastrophes averted.

Glossary

Aum Shinrikyo A Japanese religious group founded by Shoko Asahara that carried out a sarin gas attack in the Tokyo subways in 1995. The name "Aum Shinrikyo" roughly translates to "religion of truth." The group is still in existence, although it has changed its name to Aleph, and those involved in the 1995 attacks are now dead or in prison.

bioweapon Device that uses any pathogen (a bacterium, virus, or other disease-causing organism) as a weapon of war.

Bronze Star A United States armed forces military decoration that may be awarded for bravery, acts of merit, or meritorious service.

cesium-137 A radioactive isotope that is formed by nuclear fission. It is extremely toxic in minute amounts. Once released into the environment, it remains present for many years. In high enough amounts, it can cause cancer ten, twenty, or thirty years from the time of contact with the body.

cholera A severe disease caused by the bacterium *Vibrio cholerae*. Symptoms include severe diarrhea, terrible muscle and stomach cramps, vomiting, fever, and eventually, massive dehydration that can lead to death.

echelon In military terms, an echelon is a kind of staggered formation of soldiers in the field or of planes, tanks, or even cavalry. It can also mean a series of ranks or levels.

Geneva Protocol The Protocol for the Prohibition of the Use in War of Asphyxiating, Poisonous or other Gases, and of Bacteriological Methods of Warfare, usually called the Geneva Protocol, is a treaty prohibiting the first use of chemical and biological weapons. It was signed in Geneva, Switzerland, on June 17, 1925.

GI Bill (Montgomery GI Bill) The Montgomery GI Bill-Active Duty, called the MGIB for short, provides up to thirty-six months of education benefits to eligible veterans for college, technical, or vocational courses, or other training.

grunt Slang term for an infantryman in the U.S. military.

guerrilla fighters A body of fighters engaging in irregular warfare against a larger enemy.

logistics forces Groups that are responsible for planning and carrying out the movement and maintenance of military forces. They are in charge of design, development, acquisition, storage, distribution, maintenance, evacuation, and disposition of material; movement, evacuation, and hospitalization of personnel; acquisition or construction, maintenance, operation, and disposition of facilities; and acquisition or furnishing of services.

pipe bomb A simple type of improvised explosive device, consisting of a tightly sealed section of pipe filled with an explosive material. The small size of the pipe means that simple low explosives can be used to produce a relatively large explosion, and the fragmentation of the pipe itself creates potentially lethal shrapnel.

Purple Heart A military decoration awarded in the name of the president of the United States to those who have been wounded or killed while serving with the U.S. military.

reconnaissance A search made for useful military information in the field, especially by examining the ground.

Silver Star The fourth-highest military decoration that can be awarded to a member of any branch of the U.S. armed forces; given for valor in the face of the enemy.

Soviet Union The Union of Soviet Socialist Republics, also called the USSR, was a union of Socialist countries that existed in Eurasia from 1922 to 1991. Its largest member country was Russia, which contained its capital, Moscow.

triage The process of sorting victims, such as those of a battle or disaster, to determine medical priority in order to increase the number of survivors. Triage can also mean determining priorities for action in an emergency.

For More Information

Chemical Biological Incident Response Force

II Marine Expeditionary Force

3399 Strauss Avenue, Suite 219

Indian Head, MD 20640

Web site: http://cbirf.usmc.mil

The CBIRF Web site has many links for CBIRF members and for the general public, including press releases and newsletters.

The Department of Defense

Office of Public Communication

Assistant Secretary of Defense for Public Affairs

1400 Defense Pentagon

Washington, DC 20310-1400

Voice Mail: (703) 428-0711

http://www.defenselink.mil/faq

The Department of Defense's Web site provides information about the department and the military services, including FAQs, history, photos, and news.

United States Coast Guard

Coast Guard Headquarters
Commandant, U.S. Coast Guard
2100 Second Street SW
Washington, DC 20593
Web site: http://www.uscg.mil
The U.S. Coast Guard, like CBIRF, is often involved in terrorism-prevention activities, as well as search-and-rescue after natural catastrophes or terrorist attacks.

United States Marine Corps

Commandant of the Marine Corps
3000 Marine Corps
Pentagon
Washington, DC 20350-3000
(703) 614-1034
Web site: http://www.hqmc.usmc.mil
Other useful Web addresses are http://www.marines.mil and http://www.marines.com.

The Marine Corps is a large organization. For specific information about a career with the Marine Corps, you may also wish to contact your local recruiting office or spend some time on the marines.mil Web site links.

United States Navy
Chief of Information
ATTN: Department of the Navy
1200 Navy
Pentagon, Room 4B463
Washington, DC 20350-1200
Web site: http://www.navy.mil/swf/index.asp
CBIRF includes U.S. Navy officers for medical and other duties, and if that is your field of interest, you can find information about a navy career here or through a local recruiting office.

Web Sites

Due to the changing nature of Internet links, Rosen Publishing has developed an online list of Web sites related to the subject of this book. This site is updated regularly. Please use this link to access the list:

http://www.rosenlinks.com/iso/cbir

For Further Reading

Judson, Karen. *Chemical and Biological Warfare* (Open for Debate). New York, NY: Benchmark Books, 2003.

Leahy, J. F. *Honor, Courage, Commitment: Navy Boot Camp.* Annapolis, MD: U.S. Naval Institute Press, 2002.

Martin, Iain C., ed. *The Greatest U.S. Marine Corps Stories Ever Told: Unforgettable Stories of Courage, Honor, and Sacrifice.* Guilford, CT: The Lyons Press, 2007.

Pushies, Fred. *The Complete Book of U.S. Special Operations Forces.* Osceola, WA: Zenith Press, 2004.

Ricks, Thomas. *Making the Corps.* New York, NY: Scribner, 1998.

Voeller, Edward, and G. F. Marte. *U.S. Marine Corps Special Forces: Recon Marines* (Warfare and Weapons). Mankato, MN: Capstone Press, 2000.

Weinberg, Leonard, and William Lee. *What Is Terrorism?* (The Roots of Terrorism). New York, NY: Chelsea House Publications, 2006.

Bibliography

Aaseng, Nathan. *The Marine Corps in Action.* Berkeley Heights, NJ: Enslow Publishers, Inc., 2001.

Braymen, Gail. "USNORTHCOM Hosts Elite Response Team Leaders." Northcom.mil. October 2, 2006. Retrieved September 2007 (http://www.northcom.mil/News/2006/100206b.html).

Broyles, Janell. *Chemical and Biological Weapons in a Post-9/11 World.* New York, NY: Rosen Publishing, 2005.

CNNInteractive. "Oklahoma City Tragedy: The Bombing." 1996. Retrieved September 2007 (http://www.cnn.com/US/OKC/bombing.html).

CNNInteractive. "Olympic Park Bombing." 1996. Retrieved September 2007 (http://www.cnn.com/US/9607/27/olympic.bomb.main/index.html).

Dalke, Kate. "Marine Unit Battles Bioterrorism." Medill News Service. 2001. Retrieved September 2007 (http://www.medillnewsdc.com/hazmatsuit.shtml).

DCMilitary.com "NSF Indian Head: U.S. Marine Corps Chemical Biological Incident Response Force." 2007. Retrieved September 2007 (http://www.dcmilitary.com/ special_sections/sw/020607_IH/ss_113616_31938.shtml).

Ember, Lois R. "FBI Takes Lead in Developing Counterterrorism Effort." *Chemical and Engineering News*. November 4, 1996. Retrieved September 2007 (http://pubs.acs.org/hotartcl/ cenear/961104/fbi.html).

Erwin, Sandar I. "Marines Expanding Homeland Defense, Anti-Terrorism Roles." *National Defense*. January 2002. Retrieved September 2007 (http://www. nationaldefensemagazine. org/issues/2002/Jan/Marines_Expanding.htm).

GlobalSecurity.org. "Chemical/Biological Incident Response Force." 2005. Retrieved September 2007 (http://www. globalsecurity.org/military/agency/usmc/cbirf.htm).

Knight, Judson. "Chemical Biological Incident Response Force, United States." EspionageInfo.com. Retrieved September 2007 (http://www.espionageinfo.com/Ch-Co/Chemical-Biological-Incident-Response-Force-United-States.html).

Landau, Elaine. *Chemical and Biological Warfare*. New York, NY: Lodestar Books, 1991.

McMeen, Chad E. "Responding to Terrorism: CBIRF Counters Chemical and Biological Terrorist Threat." FAS.org. November 15, 1996. Retrieved September 2007 (http://fas. org/irp/news/1996/usmc961115.htm).

Princeton Review. "The Marine Corps." Retrieved September 2007 (http://www.princetonreview.com/cte/articles/military/marineoverview.asp).

Princeton Review. "The U.S. Navy." Retrieved September 2007 (http://www.princetonreview.com/cte/articles/military/navy overview.asp).

Sandhana, Lakshmi. "Plants: New Anti-Terror Weapon?" WIRED.com. April 5, 2003. Retrieved September 2007 (http://www.wired.com/science/discoveries/news/2003/04/58118).

Sands, Amy. "Biological Terrorism Poses a Serious Threat." James D. Torr, ed. *Weapons of Mass Destruction: Opposing Viewpoints*. Farmington Hills, MI: Thompson Gale, 2005.

ScienceDaily. "Wasps: Man's New Best Friend! Entomologists Train Insects to Act Like Sniffing Dogs." July 1, 2006. Retrieved September 2007 (http://www.sciencedaily.com/videos/2006/0702-wasps_mans_new_best_friend.htm).

SpecialOperations.com. "USMC Chemical-Biological Incident Response Force (CBIRF)." 2000. Retrieved September 2007 (http://www.specialoperations.com/USMC/CBIRF/default.html).

Index

About the Author

Janell Broyles is a writer and editor who lives and works in Dallas, Texas. She has written several books for Rosen Publishing, including *Chemical and Biological Weapons in a Post-9/11 World* and *Careers in Forensics: Ballistics*.

Photo Credits

Cover, cover (inset) p. 1 Marines/DOD; p. 4 © Tokyo Shimbun/Corbis Sygma; p. 7 © Time-Life Pictures/Getty Images; pp. 11, 13, 18, 22, 34, 37 © Getty Images; pp. 15, 46, 51 © AFP/Getty Images; pp. 27, 43 © AP Photos; p. 28 © John VanHasselt/Corbis Sygma; p. 31 © AFP/Getty Images; p. 47 © John Hayes/Reuters/Corbis.

Designer: Les Kanturek; **Editor:** Peter Herman
Photo Researcher: Marty Levick